The Tragic Clowns-An Analysis of the Short Lives of John Belushi, Lenny Bruce, and Chris Farley-

By Joe Guse

Foreword

When I moved to Chicago in 1997 I had only one goal, and that was to become a famous comedian like Chris Farley. Having drifted in and out of several colleges, I finally found that The Second City in Chicago was *the* place to study comedy, and with that in mind I packed my bags and moved to Chicago to study improvisational theatre. Walking into the Second City for the first time is an awe striking experience. Seeing the pictures on the wall of all the great comedians that have studied and performed there, you can't help but feel there is a kind of magic there. I met Chris Farley a couple of days before his death, when he came into a bar I worked at and began ordering drinks for everyone in the place. I told him about my plans, and he was very encouraging and couldn't have been more humble and friendly. Meeting him meant a great deal to me, and when he died just a few short days after that conversation I was heartbroken by the loss.

This experience also got me thinking a great deal about my own life. I had attempted to imitate Chris in every sense of the word, and seeing him die so young was a wake up call that would eventually send me on the road to becoming a clinical psychologist. Although I often miss those days as a comic and bartender in Chicago, Chris Farley's death triggered something in me that I knew I needed to address. This work explores many of the issues comedians may suffer through including the need to constantly entertain people, and many of the conclusions drawn in this book are as much relevant to my own life as to the lives of these three great men. I hope by exploring some of the behavioral patterns comedians often experience, I can shed further light on why men such as this often engage in such self-destructive behavior

Introduction

The "guru" of the Second City was for many years a man named Del Close who would be a mentor to both Chris Farley and John Belushi, and under his guidance both men skyrocketed to stardom. I also had the privilege of studying under Close at the Improve Olympic in Chicago, and his influence on me, as well as the field of comedy was truly far-reaching. In the movie *Wired* which depicts John Belushi's life, a notable scene occurs when Close screams at a young and impressionable John Belsuhi to "Attack the stage" and in that moment you can begin to see how Belushi began to focus his manic energy. Farley also credited Close's advice to "attack the stage" as the best advice he had ever gotten as an actor, and it comes as no surprise to many that Farley also idolized and wanted to emulate Belushi.

If there was one man who was an indisputable link between these three great comedians it was absolutely Del Close. Close was a friend of Lenny Bruce, and greatly admired his all-out rejection of traditional American values and mores. Like Lenny Bruce, Close embraced the world of drugs and found they contributed to his art and creativity. Close saw Lenny Bruce as a kind of prophet of the beat generation, and he encouraged John Belushi to take drugs, and even did them with him on several occasions when he was Belushi's director. Many years after Belushi's death, Close took a young Chris Farley under his wing, and one wonders how much Close's lifelong embrace of drugs and counterculture influenced a young and impressionable Chris Farley, as this man was the guru to his idol John Belushi. Certainly his advice to both Belushi and Farley to "attack the stage" and "cut the demons loose" made a lasting impression, and under his tutelage both of these men found a new level of comedic energy.

So where did this passion to "attack the stage" ultimately come from? Farley and Belushi's manic energy are both interesting to consider in light of Alfred Adler's (1937) comment that "The greater the feeling of inferiority that has been experienced, the more powerful is the urge to conquest and the more violent the emotional agitation." Perhaps their mania was a way of dealing with this intense emotional agitation, and this is a concept that will be examined throughout this work.

The inclusion of Lenny Bruce in this work may seem odd to some, but after reading this book I hope you see some commonalities in the lives of all three men that validates the choice to include Lenny Bruce in the conversation with these other more recent comedians. There is in fact many indisputable links in the lives of these three men, with perhaps the most obvious being they all died of drug overdoses as a result of lives of extreme excess. Beyond this link this work will attempt to show how each man's need to use drugs to such excess had reasons that went well beyond their hedonistic urges.

This book will explore the intense loneliness each of these men felt throughout their lives, and how this loneliness contributed to a maladaptive lifestyle. In exploring this loneliness this work will examine patterns of thinking that develop in childhood that contribute to feelings of loneliness, and examine these patterns in each of these three men. The book will also examine how these men escaped this loneliness by engaging in drugs, and why three such talented and popular men often seemed so terribly alone.

The most noticeable similarity between these three men is that they were all very funny, and all felt an almost constant need to entertain people. Many comedians feel and act as if they are in fact always on stage, and begin to define their worth based on the response they get from their respective crowds. This is often because comedians have learned through many childhood experiences that the best way for them to find belonging in the crowd is in essence to become the clown. The need for belonging is one of the most powerful forces in human nature, and once this belonging is found, it is not easily relinquished. The early lives of many comedians often reveal a great deal of pain, and humor is often the way this pain is crystallized and made sense of, which is usually a healthy adaptation.

The use of humor can become unhealthy when it hurts others, or alternatively it is turned excessively against the self. In the case of all three of these men, their humor had at least some relationship to their own self-loathing. While Farley is the most noticeable example of this, it also appears often in looking at the work of Belushi and Bruce. In Farley's case, playing the "Fat Clown" was a role he couldn't escape, and ultimately dramatically influenced his ability to get close to other human beings. In Lenny Bruce's case the idea proffered by Alfred Adler (1937) that "It is easier to fight for one's principles than to live up to them" was especially relevant. Bruce attacked liars and hypocrites on the stage, although he was often pathologically dishonest himself. Although he has achieved iconic status for his work on the stage, it is also interesting to consider his work as a sublimation of his own feelings of hatred towards himself. This is another theme this book will explore.

Another obvious commonality between these three men concerns their excessive drug use and eventual early deaths by drug overdose. This book will explore this drug use and examine how this use was related in part to needing to remain "on" and provide constant entertainment to the audiences in their lives. Beyond this, their use of drugs as an escape from loneliness and boredom will be examined. Although they all certainly became addicted to drugs at various points in their careers, this work will attempt to examine their drug abuse as something that went far beyond physical addiction.

One thing that often accompanies an addiction to drugs is a downward social drift, where people may start to spend time with people they would normally not associate with because of their access to drugs. Each of these three men certainly experienced this downward social drift, and in Belushi and Farley's case their last words were both to women who they barely knew, and whose only association to these men was a common interest in doing drugs. In Farley and Belushi's case their last words "Don't leave" said to a heroin addict and a stripper respectively were especially sad, and explain a great deal about these highly entertaining men who also both felt intensely alone.

Lenny Bruce

Lenny Bruce was an iconoclast like no other. He consistently challenged the norms and sacred cows of his generation, and in doing so made much of America seriously question the hypocrisy of things they once held to be beyond question. Bruce was in fact so controversial that he was arrested several times after his performances, and these arrests seriously impacted his ability to perform and spread his message. With the assistance of Hugh Hefner, Bruce published his book *How to Talk Dirty and Influence People,* (1971) where he discussed his legal problems, and continued to defy American conventions and challenge views of what society deemed as moral. His courage to confront and attack traditional mores greatly influenced current comedians such as Bill Maher, George Carlin, and Jon Stewart, whose comedy often confronts the hypocrisy in our political system to such an extent as to actually influence political elections.

The man the world came to know as Lenny Bruce was born Leonard Alfred Schneider (Goldman 1971) October 13, 1925 in Long Island, New York to Mickey and Sally Schneider. Mickey was an average man with average ambitions, but Sally was another story entirely. Having won a beauty contest at the age of 12, she developed an urge to perform that would stay with her for the rest of her life. When Lenny was 8, Sally became bored with her Long Island existence and went to Reno to get a divorce from Mickey. Following this divorce Lenny was shuffled between parents during his early years, staying mostly with his father who was the more responsible of the two. When Lenny did see his mother it was usually part of some whirlwind affair, and Lenny began to see Sally as his friend and playmate as opposed to a mother figure. Lenny officially left Long Island at the age of 17 to join the Navy, and during this experience he began to emulate his mother's performances and came to be regarded as the unofficial "entertainer" of his battalion of men.

During this same time period, Sally was beginning her career as a comedienne and had begun working the clubs in New York City under the stage name Sally Marr while making a new best friend named Sally Barton who was also an entertainer. During his time in the Navy, Lenny reconnected with his mother, and with his mother's approval began a sexual affair with Sandy Barton, who Lenny would later describe as his first true love. The three of them spent a great deal of time together during this time period with Sally playing the role of jokester and friend to Lenny during this period of early adulthood. Lenny wanted so badly to get out of the Navy at this time that he begun to impersonate a homosexual, even going so far as to tell the ship's doctors that he was obsessed with homosexual thoughts, who then recommended he be dishonorably discharged which finally occurred in October of 1945.

Following his release from the Navy, Lenny reestablished contact with Sandy and Sally. Two important things happened during this time period, one being that Lenny proposed to Sandy, and the second being that Lenny decided to be an entertainer. Lenny's mother Sally strongly objected to Lenny marrying Sandy, and this was the beginning of the end for this relationship. During this same period Mickey Schneider returned home from World War 2 and upon his return moved to Los Angeles and built two homes, one for himself and one for Lenny who he now wanted to start a father-son business with. Lenny rejected this idea and began studying acting in Los Angeles. Lenny had very little success in Los Angeles and moved back to New York to be close to his mother and pursue his entertainment career closer to home. During this period Lenny met and eventually married Honey Harlowe in 1951 and they had a daughter Kitty, four years later in 1955.

Lenny did not stand out during his early career as an entertainer (Bruce, 1965) as his routines which were based heavily on his mother's influence were old-fashioned and out of date. This changed when he met Joe Ancis (Thomas 1989) who was known as a very "sick" comic who despite his influence on other comics never performed professionally throughout his career. The shocking, grotesque, taboo-busting material Joe would talk about was highly entertaining to Lenny, and he slowly began to emulate Joe and work some of this material into his own routine. Lenny was in fact braver than Joe in some sense, as Joe was afraid to fail in public whereas Lenny could stand the rejection and keep getting back up on stage. Lenny began getting bolder and bolder on stage and at one point walked on stage naked while working in a burlesque club to emphasize the point that nudity was nudity. During this time he also became friendly with a number of Jazz musicians who first introduced Lenny to the world of drugs, which he would become addicted to and which would lead to his eventual death. His wife Honey Harlowe also became addicted to drugs, and Lenny soon filed for divorce from Honey based on her addiction and her lack of care for their daughter Kitty.

Following Lenny's split from Honey, he concentrated all of his energies into his performances, and this focus helped launch the most creative period of his career. His big break came when a club owner tried to book his mother for an appearance, who informed the club owner that it was in fact her son who deserved this golden opportunity. Lenny's subsequent performances, where he ranted against organized religion, government, and sexual politics was soon noticed by major journalists who began writing about this new ground-breaking comic who dared to talk about things previously untouched by other comics. Lenny was in fact so controversial and shocking that he was eventually arrested on obscenity charges, and due to the following legal controversy he had a great deal of trouble finding jobs during the later part of his career. During this period of his life he continued to abuse drugs, and the last years of his life were a downward spiral of drug addiction and legal battles ending with his death at the age of 40 from a heroin overdose that evidence suggests may have been intentional. Although Lenny's death attracted some media coverage and mild interest, the full legacy of his impact and influence would not be felt for many years. His refusal to compromise and conform to traditional standards cost him everything, and many consider him to be an absolute martyr for the cause of free speech in America, whose influence helped breed generations of new iconoclasts willing to question and confront mainstream American values.

Analysis

Gender Role Preparation perceived through Gender Guiding Lines and Role Models

Growing up during the depression was difficult for the Schneider family, and Lenny's father was quick to point out to Lenny the value of a dollar. His father constantly reminded Lenny that he himself would go without so his son could have things, and Lenny therefore began to assimilate the idea that a man puts his family's needs before his own. His parents divorce also has a great deal of influence on him, and his father's sense of responsibility and his mother's subsequent foray into the world of entertainment seemed to lead him to believe that men were meant to follow and enforce rules, whereas women are the source of fun and pleasure in life. Lenny eventually came to despise his father, and his desire to defy the rules in his life may have been a direct rebellion against his perception of his father's overly authoritarian ways.

It's hard to fully grasp the nature of his mother's influence on Lenny. His idea that "women provide the fun" in life, was reinforced all throughout his life, as his mother was always entertaining him and bringing him gifts, even when he rarely saw her. Conversely his father became for him the source of all that was unhappy and not fun in life, and, after sensing Lenny's disapproval with him, his father began to badly spoil Lenny. The more Lenny's father tried to win his approval, the more Lenny rejected him, and he eventually separated almost completely from his father, rejecting his "benevolent authoritarianism" in favor of his permissive and entertaining mother.

There was also some evidence (Goldman 1971) that this rejection of the masculine guiding line influenced and confused Lenny's perception of sexuality. This sexual confusion may have manifested itself when Lenny masqueraded as a homosexual to receive his discharge from the Navy. A psychologist who contributed to Goldman's (1971) book on Bruce posited the idea that this may very well have been an experimentation of his homosexual urges, and this seems possible given Lenny's early rejection of his father's guiding principles.

Interpersonal Style perceived through Experience of Family Atmosphere

Lenny's early family atmosphere consisted of very little harmony between his father's respect for rules and conformity and his mother's need for constant amusement and entertainment. In this capacity Lenny's mother was also very dishonest with his father, and her dishonesty and her husband's subsequent mistrust both influenced the young Leonard Schneider. She describes herself as a "prisoner" when she was stuck at home, and she would often go out and perform at amateur nights despite the protests of her disapproving husband. All of this led to a kind of "stormy" family atmosphere that young Lenny interpreted as the fault of his father. Interestingly in an interview with Mickey Schneider, he explains to journalist Albert Goldman (1971) that Lenny had "an abundance of love" growing up, and Mr. Schneider strongly contested Lenny's later claims that he was an ogre and a tyrant obsessed with the rules when he was young.

Lenny models this early pattern of storm and strife throughout his life and all his interpersonal relationships essentially mimic this early parental pattern of intensity and then disconnection. This is even true of Lenny's relationship with his audience, where he essentially began to sabotage his own performances late in his career, and may have been rejecting his audiences before they had a chance to reject him.

Personal Code of Conduct perceived through Acceptance / Rejection of Family Values

In researching Lenny Bruce's early life, it seemed that there was very little about anything that his parents agreed upon, and it is even suggested that they would never have even been married except for the fact that Sally lied about being pregnant. Goldman (1971) suggests Sally did this because she desired a strong motherly relationship with Mickey's mother, whom she was very close to. Sally's own mother was committed to a mental institution when Sally turned 18 and this event left a void in Sally's life that she temporarily filled by marrying Mickey. Mickey, who was also close to his own mother who was indisputably in charge of her own household, also stressed to Lenny the importance of the maternal relationship, and therefore an important family value was taught to Lenny, that the mother was a figure who should be respected and revered. This matriarchal society had in fact been a theme in Lenny's heritage for a couple of generations, and undoubtedly influenced the kind of blinding loyalty and admiration he felt for his mother.

Interestingly, Lenny rejected this family value in his own dealings with his wife and daughter, and instead chose to mimic his father's actions regarding his own daughter. When Lenny divorced Honey because he thought she was an unfit mother, he made the decision that he would be the one who would care for their daughter. This choice was in many ways similar to the one his father made, and reflected his father's thinking that men were the ones who took responsibility in times of crisis. This new dynamic seemed to start with Lenny's father following his divorce and this decision to care for his daughter seemed to be the one firm choice in his life that was influenced by his father's family values.

Perspective on the World perceived through Experience of Psychological Birth Order

Lenny was an only child in a time and place where big families were the norm. The fact that Lenny's mother tricked his father into marrying her by pretending to be pregnant may have cast an unusual shadow over Lenny's life, and may explain in part the strained relationship between Lenny and his father. Loneliness is a common symptom found in only children, and this was certainly true of Lenny, who gravitated to the drug culture in part because of this persistent loneliness and desire to belong to part of a family. For Lenny this sense of belonging was found amongst the beatnik crowd in New York who found a common bond through music and drugs. Only children are often the center of their parent's universe, and despite her absenteeism, Lenny's mother definitely showered Lenny with praise throughout his life which seemed to give him the confidence he needed to perform in front of hundreds and even thousands of people. Only children also often have a sense of uniqueness where they may have difficulty seeing that others might see the world as they do. In Lenny's case this often prevented him from getting close to people in his life, and this seemed to affect his ability to sustain intimate relationships beyond the purely sexual

Self Assessment perceived through Genetic Possibilities

Lenny was a very small baby (Bruce 1965) who was always smaller than the other kids growing up.

Because of his short stature he learned to live on his wits, and even as a child was clever at compensating for his small stature by outsmarting and outthinking the other children. Lenny's view of himself as a "little" person greatly influenced his future ambitions. He seems to have concluded that if he couldn't be the "biggest" person physically, than he would show the others by being bigger in terms of his verbal acuity and influence. Essentially he became "big" by learning how to seize attention and control from others by becoming the "mouth that roared." This sense of being able to live on his wits stayed with Lenny when he entered the Navy at the age of 17, where despite his smaller stature he avoided confrontation and became popular by being the class clown of his unit. Here again, despite his short stature, he has become the "biggest" person in his group by entertaining the others and gaining power with his personality and ability to entertain. This pattern is repeated often in Lenny's life, and can even be seen in his conquests of women (Bruce 1964), where despite not being as physically large as other men, he competed through the use of personality and charm, and again adjusted for his lack of physical size with his words and courage.

Openings for Advancement perceived through Environmental Opportunities

Lenny's upbringing provided an opportunity to develop a sense of adaptability and an ability to think quickly on his feet. Because he was so often shuffled around from home to home, he seems to have concluded that he had to quickly learn and assimilate the patterns of each new household he was thrust into, and this ability to improvise and adapt was of great assistance to him onstage as a performer. Due to his mother's influence, Lenny was also able to hang around comedy clubs at a young age and observe the mechanisms and mannerisms of many different performers which helped him cultivate his stage presence at a very young age. Goldman (1971) also describes how, despite the depression Lenny's father saved enough to but Lenny a dictionary and a set of encyclopedias which he quickly became obsessed with. Semantics and language would later become the cornerstone of Lenny's social commentary, and this is an interesting connection given his early obsession with memorizing and learning the meaning of new words.

All of these circumstances helped Lenny develop the verbal acumen, confidence, poise, and experience to become a performer. In particular Lenny's mother's influence helped provide Lenny with opportunities for achievement, and this was particularly true when she gave up a personal chance to get her big break by instead convincing the owner of a big comedy club that Lenny would be a much better headliner for the show. Aside from his mother, Lenny's early experiences in comedy clubs helped him develop contacts that would benefit him throughout his life, and this early environmental opportunity proved particularly useful to him as his career advanced.

Range of Social Interest perceived through Other Particularities

Lenny's Jewish heritage was absolutely essential to his comedy, the way he viewed the world, and the way he gave and received love. Goldman (1971) describes a phenomenon called "Jewish Love" with regards to Lenny, and he talks about how Jewish love differs from Gentile love in that it is a positive emotion where a number of inherent negative qualities are also implied such as condescension and guilt. This speaks directly to his relationship with his father, who when he gave Lenny something always reminded him that it was possible because he had chosen "to do without" so Lenny could have. Oddly Lenny forgave everyone in his life except his father, and he eventually began to view their early interactions as responsible for much of his later maladaptive behavior. In his comedy routines Lenny alternatively mocked and celebrated his Jewish heritage, and the influence of the different Jewish relatives in his life all provided him with ample ethnic material that he would draw upon for the entirety of his career.

Socially Lenny was greatly influenced by the comedians his mother hung around with, and also more generally by the Beatnik way of life that was beginning to take shape during the early part of his comedy career. As a young man watching this behavior convinced Lenny that a life that included promiscuity and drugs was an acceptable alternative to mainstream American ideas, and these early influences dramatically shaped his future lifestyle. Economically, through his interactions with his father Lenny saw that money had strings attached to it. When his father gave him something it was always accompanied by feelings of guilt, and this followed Lenny throughout his entire career. When he received financial offers that were on the surface fantastic opportunities, he always found himself mistrusting people's motivations and wondering when the other shoe was going to drop.

This basic mistrust of others learned from his early interactions with his father, and his inability to establish intimacy with others, learned through his interactions with his mother, dramatically affected Lenny's ability to develop a sense of social interest. Lenny therefore descended even further into his loneliness, and continued to escape from his loneliness by spiraling deeper and deeper into the world of drugs.

Lenny also developed the mind of criminal at a very a young age in accordance with his rejection of the principles of social interest. In his autobiography he talks about stealing bottles for extra money, and this early behavior would blossom into a lifelong pattern of trying to "get over" on others and get the best deal for himself. This was clearly demonstrated when Lenny posed as a priest during his time in Florida in his youth, where he eventually scammed many people, including a number of elderly women out of almost 8,000 dollars by posing as a priest and then securing donations from them after praying on their sympathies and providing comfort to them as fake priest.

Although this story is presented in Lenny's autobiography as a humorous anecdote, it represents a lifelong pattern of the rejection of social interest in other people. This pattern often begins in childhood, when a rejected and isolated child, who feels unwanted by the world, begins to adopt an "I'll get the before they get me" mentality and acts accordingly. Lenny's lack of trust in other people and his lifelong pursuit of cons and scams that he performed well after it was financially necessary; all have their roots in the lack of trust Lenny had in other human beings that was established during his youth.

Summary

In conceptualizing the life of Lenny Bruce, it is useful to use an Adlerian model (Powers and Griffith 1974) that examines impressions gained from a client's story. In Lenny Bruce's case his need to belong, which may have had its origins in the fact that he was the only child of divorced parents, led to his finding acceptance in a world full of friends who abused some very dangerous drugs, One wonders if Lenny may have drifted towards people with similar difficulties with intimacy and loneliness whose strongest bond may have been this shared desire to escape from their sense of loneliness. In any case Lenny seems to have found belonging by abusing drugs with his new "family" and this decision led to his addiction to narcotics which was a demon that haunted him for the rest of his life.

Lenny also had difficulties with trust that were developed in childhood, as following his parent's divorce he was often unsure if he could count on and depend on them. This inability to trust followed him throughout his life, and he often overcompensated for this by sleeping with women strangers and then moving on to others seemingly before there was a chance for some kind of trustful intimacy to develop. Because he was unable to develop intimate relationships, his lifelong feelings of loneliness were exacerbated, and he drifted further into his escapist world of drug abuse.

There was also a very large issue in Lenny's life of wanting to please and emulate his mother. The family value of the women being the voice of authority seemed especially relevant to Lenny's life, as despite his mother's flaky and aloof behavior, he still chose to emulate her as opposed to his father, which would seem to be a more logical choice for a young heterosexual male. Lenny in fact placed his mother on such a pedestal that he thought nothing of her abandoning him for long stretches of time, and instead chose to turn his anger on his father who made great sacrifices to see that Lenny was financially cared for. Interestingly Lenny (Bruce 1965) describes his first comic inspiration as beginning shortly after his parent's divorce, and therefore the onset of this need to identify with his mother seemed to have begun at that point.

Related to this idea are the beliefs Lenny cultivated as related to his gender guiding lines and the private logic he developed along with these guiding lines. Lenny began to dichotomize his relationship with his parents, coming to see his father as all bad and his mother as all good. This reaction to his father may have directly shaped his desire to thumb his nose at the rules, and his almost violent rebellion against any kind of rules and values seemed to be an overcompensation of the anger he felt towards his father. At its core, Lenny's life and work seemed to constantly and consistently attack men in powerful positions who he believed were hypocrites and liars.

Despite the fact that Lenny was often brutally and shockingly honest on stage (Goldman 1971) he was described by his friends as almost pathologically dishonest in his personal life. This is interesting to consider in terms of Lenny's violent hatred of the lies that he believed were at the base of many American values. From an Adlerian perspective, it seems possible that young Lenny, who observed an early family atmosphere where dishonesty was rampant, began to model this behavior, while also understanding that these lies were dangerous and disruptive to the family. Perhaps he understood on some level how dishonesty helped contribute to his unhappy childhood, while also emulating this quality in his mother for whom dishonesty came very naturally and was a regular part of her interactions with others.

Lenny's own pattern of self-loathing and low opinion of family life was confirmed by the fact that during their time together Honey aborted six children so she and Lenny could continue their hedonistic lifestyle. Lenny insisted on these abortions, as he felt having a baby would cramp the swinging lifestyle he and Honey had created for themselves. Certainly these excessive abortions and overall disrespect for human life reflect Lenny's own distaste for human life, and his desire to "not inflict another Lenny Bruce on the world" clearly speaks to his own feelings about himself as well as his place in the world.

In terms of how Lenny's mother influenced his life, it is absolutely fascinating to consider his mother's career as a comedienne, which was a highly unusual and unconventional career choice for a woman raised at the beginning of the twentieth century. Sally's own life was quite groundbreaking, as her decision to forgo the life of raising a family to pursue a career in entertainment was a tremendously rebellious act for that place and time. It is also useful to consider his mother's Histrionic personality in this regard, and how her own difficulties with intimacy may have come directly as a result of her interactions with her own mother. It seems likely that because his mother never had an effective mother child relationship in her own life, that she was therefore unable to develop this kind of relationship with her own child. Therefore because Lenny chose to identify with his mother, he seemed to inherit a number of Sally's Histrionic traits, including the development of superficial relationships which Goldman (1971) confirms by reporting that Sally had virtually no true friends due to her overwhelming need to constantly entertain people. Like many Histrionics, both Sally and Lenny were both seemingly very popular people who were in fact very lonely and isolated on the inside, as everyone in their worlds became part of an audience that they must provide entertainment for.

Further interactions between Sally and Lenny throughout their life provided some rich irony in their relationship. In one of Lenny's early movies called *Dreamfollies* Lenny cast himself in the role of the henpecked husband, and none other than his mother in the role of his nagging wife. One wonders if this wasn't an attempt to recreate elements in his childhood where he created a story where the mother actually takes an interest in the family, even to the point of becoming overbearing. Perhaps this represented Lenny's desire for traditional maternal guidance, and there is of course the Freudian overtone of casting your own mother as your wife.

Concerning this sexual dynamic, Goldman (1974) discusses how Lenny's problems were at least in part a result of wanting to escape the sexual advances of his mother. This idea is interesting to consider, as Sally eventually married a man 10 years younger than Lenny, and then attempted to mold him into the next Lenny Bruce. It seems clear that because Sally's own husband did not provide the excitement she craved from a partner, that she clearly got a great deal of this excitement from Lenny. In any case there seemed to be a lot of confusing sexual feelings in the dynamic between Sally and Lenny, and this confusion certainly affected both of their intimate relationships throughout their lives.

Lenny certainly married a woman much like his mother. Like Sally, Honey was an entertainer who was highly irresponsible and became easily bored by the trappings of domestic life. Lenny and Honey's marriage had some similarities to his parents, but this time Lenny seized the power so as not to relive his earlier childhood pain. Because he feared Honey would abandon him like his mother did, he instead chose to destroy the marriage before she had a chance too, and this again seems to be a repetition of a familiar pattern in Lenny's life.

The period of Lenny's life following his split with Honey can be interestingly conceived through the use of the theory of object relations. This theory suggests that we make mental representations of people that stay in out heads and influence the way we live. In Lenny's case, Honey became the audience he played for in the most creative period in his career, and he was able to sublimate his rage towards her to become highly focused and productive.

Because Lenny had developed a number of maladaptive behavior patterns based on his interpretation of childhood experiences, it would have been very difficult for him to develop healthier patterns without sacrificing some of his comic genius. One way he may have accomplished this would have been to draw on the many resources he had developed and begin to reexamine some of the fictions he had created for himself to develop healthier modes of living. One of Lenny's strengths and resources was courage, and perhaps he could have learned to draw on this courage and confront and gain insight into some of his personal demons. He may then have come to understand that he was strong enough to face life without escaping into drugs, and this realization may have in fact saved his life. Lenny was also exceptionally creative as well as adaptable, and a psychologist may have been able to draw on these strengths to help him create a fiction that helped him understand that his life could still be meaningful without having to constantly be engaged in a battle to defy and confront authority.

Lenny clearly had mental representations of his parents and in particular his father that he constantly played to throughout his life. His father for him became the embodiment of everything he despised in his life, and many of Lenny's railings on the stage can be seen as a direct response to his childhood pain. In reinterpreting Lenny's difficulty, it would have been very instructive to hold a mirror up that reflected to him how his need to defy his authoritarian father and please his histrionic mother influenced his decisions as an adult. This insight may have led to a recognition reflex for Lenny where he came to understand that much of his behavior was influenced by this one firmly entrenched pattern of behavior.

If Lenny had been able to create some new fictions in his life, he might have been able to begin to see how life was not simply made up of the dichotomies that seemed to dominate his thinking and strongly influence his behavior. He could then have developed some less self-destructive goals, and come to understand that as a parent and a comic, he was much more valuable to the world living past the age of 40, which was much too young for a man of his considerable creativity and influence to die.

In conclusion, Lenny Bruce's life and work influenced many people, and he certainly helped reinvent the idea of free speech in America. The tragedy of Lenny's life was that many of the things that made him great also led to his eventual self-destruction. Although it is easy to celebrate and applaud Lenny's accomplishments, his life was also very tragic and sad, and there is an important lesson to be learned form his short time here on earth. Lenny's life truly blurred the lines between tragedy and comedy, and although he left a powerful and lasting legacy behind, his was a life undoubtedly lived with little insight or perspective.

John Belushi

John was a clown, indeed, in the Shakespearean sense, which is to say he was utterly imbued with a feeling of both the joy and the sadness of being human"

William Styron

John Belushi was one of the most manic and high-energy comedians the world has ever known. When he burst onto the scene on Saturday Night Live in the 1970s America was immediately captivated by his magnetism and charm, and he quickly parlayed this interest into a successful movie career. The movies *Animal House* and *The Blues Brothers* quickly became huge hits, and the legend of John Belushi began to grow. As John's fame continued to grow, so did his appetites for newer and better highs. When John died of a drug overdose in 1983, people around America were deeply saddened if not totally surprised. John's life was documented in fellow Wheaton, Illinois native Bob Woodward's book *Wired* which was later made into a movie. This book, and later the movie were highly controversial and many people, including John's wife Judy, felt the book over emphasized the dark side of John Belushi, without providing a full appreciation of his many positive traits.

John Belushi was born January 24, 1949 in Wheaton Illinois. Wheaton is considered to be one of the most religious cities in America, and was also the birthplace of the reverend Billy Graham. John's parents were John (Adam) and Agnes Belushi, who were immigrants from Albania who moved to America with the dream of providing a better life for their family. John was the second of four

Belushi children, and the first born male in the family that also included an older sister Marian, and two younger brothers Jim and Billy.

Adam was a resterauntuer in the Chicago area, and was rarely home during Belushi's childhood which meant he was often disciplined by his mother Agnes and grandmother Nena who also lived in the home. John was a popular child, and although he looked very different from the other kids in Wheaton, he quickly became popular by becoming the class clown of the group. Realizing the power of humor, John purchased comedy albums by his early idol Jonathon Winters as well as Bob Newhart and he listened to them over and over trying to copy the mannerisms and speech of these comedians. John found early belonging through the use of humor, and expanded on this by becoming an actor in the school plays where he quickly became a standout performer. John was eventually voted both class clown as well as homecoming King in High School, where he was also an excellent football player.

Following High School, John continued his acting career and got a job as an actor doing summer stock that paid 50 dollars a week. Following this he went to College and during this time John became more politically conscious and even took place in the infamous Chicago Democratic convention in 1968 where he was shot by teargas by the National Guard which made a lasting impression on him. During this same period John saw his first show at the legendary Second City in Chicago, and he quickly returned there as often as he could, often memorizing the scenes from the show and then performing them with his classmates back at school. John formed the West Compass players shortly after this, and many of the scenes he created during this time involved police brutality and other anti-establishment material.

It was also during this period where John first started experimenting with drugs, and his rejection and then gradual acceptance of drugs is documented by a series of letters he wrote to his then girlfriend Judy that is documented in her autobiography Samurai Widow (1986). John's early struggle then acceptance of drugs will reflect a lifelong pattern of resistance and then surrender with drugs, and this acceptance was certainly a catalyst for many of John's later problems.

The next phase of John's career took place at the Second City theatre in Chicago, and this was for the John the culmination of a dream come true. Like Lenny Bruce before him, John challenged the accepted norms of comedy while at the Second City, and he was the first one to infuse foul language into the show on a regular basis. John gained a reputation as a scene-stealer while at the Second City, and during this time he began to use more drugs including LSD. John eventually left Chicago to work in New York on a show called *Lemmings* where he worked with another budding star named Chevy Chase. Belushi and Chase almost immediately became rivals, but it was Chase who eventually convinced Lorne Michaels to give Belushi a shot as a cast member on the revolutionary not ready from prime time players at Saturday Night Live.

John's time at Saturday Night Live arguably represented the most creative of his career. It was during these years that John created his famous Samurai character, did his famous Marlon Brando impersonation, and performed with Dan Akroyd as one half of the famous Blues Brothers. During

John's early years at SNL Rolling Stone magazine did a cover piece on John calling him "The Most Dangerous Man on Television" and this article certainly increased the John Belsuhi legend.

After some turbulent times with Judy during these years, she and John eventually married and began their life together as man and wife. Judy often did drugs with John during this period, while also reminding him that he was doing them entirely too much. It was also during these years at Saturday Night Live that the script of Animal House was created, and the part of "Bluto" in the movie as the hard-drinking wild man was written with John Belushi in mind. This part made John Belushi an even bigger star, and for the rest of his career John's fans basically wanted to see a replication of the Bluto character in everything else he did. The Blues Brothers was also a huge success, and John Belushi was now a wealthy man, and had the money to obtain whatever he wanted, including very large quantities of drugs which John continued to use to excess. John, now a huge success in the entertainment business would then leave Saturday Night Live to pursue a career in movies, and this move marked the beginning of a downward spiral for John both personally and professionally.

During the final phase of John's career he made the romantic comedy *Continental Divide* with Blair Brown, which he had hoped would make him a Spencer Tracy like leading man. John began exercising when he was offered this role, and managed to stay off drugs long enough to get in shape and lose a great deal of weight to play the part. Following the wrap of this movie, John made the movie *Neighbors* with Dan Akroyd and in this movie John played the straight man to Akroyd's manic character. The movie was a critical and commercial flop, and this failure helped send John deeper and deeper into the world of drugs. John became obsessed with returning to the limelight, and he began work on a script called *Noble Rot* with Don Novello who had performed with John on Saturday Night Live. It was during this time that John began regularly using Heroin, and his constant use of drugs during this period of his life culminated in his accidental overdose on March 5th 1982. John's death shocked and deeply saddened the entertainment world, and his star-studded funeral was highlighted by James Taylor's performance of the song *That Lonesome Road* which for many put an appropriate stamp on the life of John Belushi.

Analysis

Gender Role Preparation perceived through Gender Guiding Lines and Role Models

Through his interactions with his father, John learned that hard work was the only thing that really mattered, and that time with your family came second. His father was in fact so committed to his work that the Belushi's didn't even always celebrate holidays, as these provided the best opportunity for Adam to earn money in his restaurants. Through watching his father, John learned to prioritize work in his own life, and often neglected his wife Judy to relentlessly pursue his latest project. The masculine guiding line in the Belsuhi family was therefore that money came first and that a pursuit of one's personal goals took priority over everything else in life. In this capacity a man should do whatever it takes to succeed in the life task of work, as this was truly the measure of a man's success.

With John's father away from home so often, John's mother became the disciplinarian in the family, and John learned he could often escape her discipline if he could make his mother laugh. John therefore formed an early idea that if one breaks the rules, one could escape consequences for these actions through the use of humor. This was an early lesson that John applied often throughout his life, as he often used humor to minimize his drug problems and direct people way from this topic of conversation.

John's father was not easily amused, and was the ultimate authority around the house when he was home and in these cases John's mother's authority became secondary. This pattern instilled in John a belief that women in authority were therefore not to be taken seriously, and John had difficulties working with and respecting women as equals throughout his acting career. This pattern of not taking women in authority seriously also affected John's marriage, where John took Judy's threats to leave him because of his drug abuse as empty and without validity.

Interpersonal Style perceived through Experience of Family Atmosphere

John's interpersonal style was greatly influenced by his early family interactions, as he learned that one could use avoidance to withdraw from difficult situations, as his parents had a lifelong pattern of avoiding each other that continued into old age. Although his parents never got divorced, his father would spend most nights in an apartment over his restaurant to avoid having to come home to difficulties with his wife. Later when they were adults, this pattern of avoidance continued, as John's father moved to Los Angles to live on ranch, while his mother lived in Chicago in a place that

John had purchased for her. In John's life he used avoidance almost constantly to elude conversations about his drug use, and when friends like his manager Bernie Brillstein explained to John that he was killing himself with drugs, he would avoid the topic and accuse him of meddling in his affairs. Drugs therefore became the 3,000 pound Elephant in the room with John Belushi, as he had no interest in spending time with you if you wanted to talk about his drug use, and therefore those close to him often simply chose to avoid this topic of conversation. Because people wanted access to John, and doing drugs was the quickest way to gain this access, John's close friends often enabled and provided John with drugs and even did them with him which certainly exacerbated John's addiction. (Woodward 1983.)

John therefore often drifted away from those people that truly cared about him in his life, as they were unwilling to turn a blind eye to the fact that he was killing himself. This contributed to the downward social drift in his life where he ended up most comfortable in the company of those that shared his addictions and his last words, "Don't leave" to a Heroin-addicted acquaintance like Cathy Smith certainly speaks to this phenomenon.

Personal Code of Conduct perceived through Acceptance / Rejection of Family Values

The family value of "work comes first" certainly made an impression on John and, despite his image as a fat and lazy slob evidenced by the Bluto character in Animal House, John was often a very hard worker in his life. His father's precedence on work was in fact so great that he often referred to his children numerically when assigning chores around the house. John's father wanted John to take over the family restaurant business when he was old enough, and John's refusal of this proposal fueled in John the need to prove to his father that he could be highly successful in the world in areas other than the restaurant business.

John's obsession with work also had a relationship to his drug problems. He felt that cocaine kept him sharp as a performer, and that his public expected him to be "on" all the time, which was in part the truth. Complete strangers would often give John cocaine, and even when he was trying to kick his habits, cocaine was something that was always around and readily available to John. In many ways John was a victim of his own creations, as the level of manic energy he provided on Saturday Night Live as well as in *Animal House* and The *Blues Brothers* raised a bar that he was constantly trying to replicate. John came to believe that he could only replicate this energy through the use of drugs, and this was almost certainly a mistaken belief and a bit of faulty logic on John's part. Most of those who performed with him say John was sloppy and not as affective of a performer while on drugs and that he was much funnier and talented during the periods where he was clean. John did not accept this idea, and his maniacal need to achieve and perform at a high level certainly had some of its roots in the family obsession with work and achievement that John learned from watching his father Adam.

John's obsession with work and his need to indulge in cocaine that fueled this work also dramatically affected his relationship with his wife Judy. Consider the following letter John wrote in the middle of feeling torn between having to keep up a high level of performance on Saturday Night

Live, while also maintaining a relationship with his wife Judy. From Samurai Widow (1990)-

Judy, I'm afraid of myself because of what I'm capable of doing to you. If I was the kind of person I want to be, then why do I hurt you? Is it because no one can be that person? Do I kid myself? When I fail, who am I?.........

I want to take care of you, but I feel I'm not capable. The most difficult thing to deal with is disappointing you or finding myself unable to help you. When I'm sick, you help. When you are sick, I freak. Is it because I feel helpless? What can I do? Hide in.........drugs?

Please, Please, Please don't think I'm going back to my old pattern. I may have slipped a patch, but not a pattern. What I really want is forgiveness that may not be deserved.

This letter certainly speaks to the cognitive dissonance and the inner war that was going on inside John Belushi that was fueled by his all-encompassing desire to succeed. Clearly he saw the nature of his desires were interfering with his ability to maintain happy relationships, and yet he understood there were also powerful patterns in his life that were shaped by his early experiences.

Perspective on the World perceived through Experience of Psychological Birth Order

As the first born son in a traditional Albanian family, John was psychologically the leader of the children and expected to be the one who went out into the world and provided for and took care of the family when the father was gone. The son is in fact so important in the Albanian culture, that his mother Agnes (Belsuhi-Pisano 2005) described being rejected by Adam's family with whom she and her husband lived during the War when her firstborn child was a woman and not a man. This pressure to succeed as the first born son was increased by the fact that John's parents sacrificed so their children could have a better life in America, and it is fair to say that John felt he held the fate of the Belushis squarely in his hands. This idea became especially relevant when John's father failed at the restaurant business, and John then became almost entirely responsible for financially supporting the family. This pattern of dependency on John increased as his fame and fortune rose, as his mother would often make requests for more money and other perks from John's accountants, as she quickly began to enjoy the doors that John's fame would open for her. John gave hundreds of thousands of dollars to his family over the years, and the pressures of being the first born son certainly contributed to his sense of responsibility in this regard.

John's Albanian heritage and small stature fueled a desire in John to compensate for these perceived disadvantages and become "larger than life." John was ashamed at times of being Albanian in a town like Wheaton, and he overcame this by pretending to be from Greece which was in his mind a more acceptable background. Although the other children were at first reluctant to become involved with him because of his physical differences, John quickly found he could find a sense of belonging with the other children by being the class clown and making them laugh. The origins of John Belushi's humor seems to have its roots in these early childhood experiences, as he found that with his mother, as well as with his classmates, this was a surefire way to get out of trouble.

Self Assessment perceived through Genetic Possibilities

An interesting part of John's physical comedy was developed by having to communicate with his grandmother Nena who spoke very little English who John therefore had to communicate with non-verbally. Through these communications with his grandmother John learned to express himself with his physicality, and this translated into his later gift as a physically talented comedian. John in fact did such an impressive non-verbal audition for Lorne Michael on his Saturday Night Live audition that Michaels offered him the job on the spot. It is interesting to make the connection between John's early communications with his grandmother and his later development as one of the funniest physical comedians of his generation.

John also compensated for his lack of size by becoming such a good football player that he was eventually named all-conference for the area in which he played. John's small size also helped him develop his verbal skills, and like Lenny Bruce before him, John also became in many ways "the mouth that roared." On stage John's presence truly was larger than life, and despite his small height he became "large" with his intensity, charisma, and manic energy.

Summary

One fascinating psychological insight into John Belushi's experience as a smaller person comes from analyzing his obsession with Napoleon. John truly believed that the studio often hassled him because he was such a small man, and his preoccupation with Napoleon was so great that his wife Judy recounts an incident where John sprang up in bed talking about Napoleon and declaring "I shall ride a white horse." (Belushi-Pisano 2005)

In this regard, it is interesting to think about John's life using the work of Joseph Campbell as a guide and in particular the use of the hero myth. Campbell talks about how the myth of the traveling hero is one that is found in every culture, and that individuals may also begin to see their lives as a kind of "hero" journey with themselves cast as the leading character. Campbell (1949) talks about how these stories all have some basic elements, and John's conceptualization of his life certainly seems to fit this bill.

The first of these is the "call to adventure." In this stage John left home to study the theatre, and later to New York City in search of fame and fortune. In this capacity the hero may meet someone called the "herald" (Coincidentally the name of Del Close's improv technique) who encourages the character towards his adventure, and in John's case this was certainly Del Close. Del pushed John to "cut the demons loose" in his life and without Del Close's involvement it is entirely possible John would not have become the performer he eventually became.

After this the "road of trials" came in John's life, and in this phase of the legend the hero must overcome difficulties and remerge stronger and more powerful. In John's case in his early experiences as an actor he was considered to be selfish and not a team player, and was considered by many of his colleagues to be unprofessional and overly aggressive. Not only did John not apply these criticisms to his life, he became more radiant and expressive with his work, and he was therefore able to capture the spotlight to such a degree that he eventually succeeded far beyond those that criticized him.

Women also have a place in the hero legend, and the lead character often marries a wise guiding force following the overcoming of obstacles, and John was no exception as it was during this time period that he decided to marry Judy. A female temptress may also emerge in this part of the hero legend, and John's involvement with Cathy Smith, who provided a steady stream of the demon Heroin supports this idea in John's life. She not only offered ready access to the drug, but also shot him up with Heroin and was instrumental in helping push John to his death.

Although the hero narrative is a fascinating way to conceptualize John's life, it is also impossible to talk about the life of John Belushi without talking about how severe of a drug addict he really was. Although there has been some discussion of the forces that helped compel John to do drugs, it is also useful to include a discussion on the nature of addiction.

One factor that absolutely cannot be overlooked was the relationship between Del Close and John Belushi and how this relationship influenced John's acceptance of drugs. Because John was not close to his own father and did not see him as a role model, Del Close in many ways became for John a kind of surrogate father and guiding force. Del Close felt drugs were an inspirational tool, and because his guru so readily endorsed his drug use, John may have rationalized that drugs were a necessary component of his comedy. Following his departure from the Second City, John would often go to Del Close's house where Del would inject John with speed, as in Del's words, "Junkies give the best shots." Having your mentor and guide not only endorse drug use, but actually participate in injecting you, certainly contributed to John's belief that drugs were an integral part of his work. John developed the mistaken belief that his comedy and drug use were inseparable, and during his last years on Saturday Night Live he had become severely addicted to cocaine. Because cocaine use was so rampant during this time period, people were quick to overlook John's addiction and felt that as long as he continued to perform that he would be ok.

The cycle of John's drug use was fairly typical of an addict and contained a great deal of denial. Gorski (2000) talks about denial as "The natural tendency to avoid the pain caused by recognizing the presence, severity, and responsibility for dealing with serious problems" and this definition fits very well with regard to John Belushi's life. It appears that much of John's drug use was a result of the mistaken private logic that he needed drugs to perform, and as a result of this faulty logic he became a virtual slave to his addictions. Denial is often an automatic process that begins when people experience cognitive dissonance about the problems that drugs are causing in their lives. In John's case he would abruptly change the subject when the topic of his drug use came up, and this was a reaction that was consistently documented by almost everyone who attempted to discuss this subject with him.

John certainly felt some cognitive dissonance about this, as his letters to Judy demonstrating his anguished desire to get off drugs certainly demonstrated. Holding these two conflicting thoughts together appeared to put John in a great deal of psychological pain and John escaped this pain the only way he knew how which was through the use of drugs. This self-defeating cycle almost always represents an ability to escape emotional pain, and in particular the self-attacking emotions of guilt and shame Consider these lyrics from the song "Guilty" that John performed and became especially enamored with during the Blues Brothers years-

"You know I just can't stand myself.

It takes a whole lot of medicine, darlin'

For me to pretend that I'm somebody else."

For an addict to admit he is powerless in his life over drugs is seen as a sign of incredible weakness, and someone who put the kind of pressure John Belushi did on himself to succeed could not accept that he could be this psychologically powerless. Therefore the easiest thing to do for John was to engage in self-deception and rationalize his drug use as something he could control. Although a huge part of John understood what was happening to him, the part of him that was addicted seemed to win most of the time. Del Close's admonishment to John to "let the demons out" seems to say a great deal about John's battle with his personal demons, and his repeated failures to control his urges speak directly to the faulty logic that John developed, partially through the advice and modeling of his mentor Del Close.

John's patterns of denial continued until his death despite several warning from doctors that he was killing himself. Despite these admonishments, these doctors would still often end up prescribing downers to Belushi, as, along with his cocaine addiction he also had become addicted to Quaaludes which were necessary to bring John down after an extended binge. John was often at his worst when he was working, as the interfering idea would become activated that he needed drugs to be at his best would become most prevalent during these times. These interfering ideas and thoughts would come to John during filming downtimes, and during his free time while he was anticipating a shot, John could not stand to be alone with his own thoughts and used drugs to escape from these disturbing cognitions.

Further evidence of John's cognitive dissonance towards his drug use was emphasized by the fact that he hired an ex Secret Service agent named Smokey Wendell whose sole job was to keep cocaine and other drugs away from John. Smokey would often intercept packages of cocaine that people tried to smuggle to John, and his positive influence on John's life most likely extended John's life if for even just a few years. John would often vacillate between rage and love towards Smokey, and his reactions to him were very indicative of the same war that was going on inside his own troubled mind.

Eventually Smokey Wendell moved in with John, and in his capacity as the drug enforcer he got to know John and his ideas about drugs perhaps better than anyone. Smokey described times when John would wake him up in the middle of the night to talk, and Smokey's take on this was that John's demons were always with him and would often come to him when he was feeling especially empty in the middle of the night. John admitted to Smokey that he took drugs because of the pressure of performing, and Smokey was always quick to point out the errors in John's logic which John alternatively loved him and despised him for. If anyone was ever able to hold a mirror up to John's face about his drug use, it as definitely Smokey Wendell, and when Smokey and John parted ways because John was "feeling better" it marked the beginning of yet another downward spiral for John Belushi. (Belsuhi-Pisano 2005)

In Denial Management Counseling, John's break from Smokey Wendell would be known as a "flight into health." In this stage of denial, people believe that because they are beginning to feel better that they must be totally well, and this is how John rationalized his drug use after Smokey Wendell left his life. In this stage of denial people may have developed some understanding about their addiction, and feel that this understanding and a period of abstinence means they are totally "cured" and with an addict this is never entirely possible. In John's case extensive therapy that helped him seriously examine the faulty logic that preceded his urges would have been necessary, and John's only attempt at therapy lasted just fourth months, and predictably at the end of these four months, John explained to Judy that he was now free from his addictions.

Conclusion

The life of John Belsuhi was truly the life of the sad clown. Despite the fact that John made millions of people laugh throughout his life, there was something inside of him that never quite let him feel happy enough to enjoy his own success. Harold Ramis described this as the "Imposter syndrome" where a person never quite believes that they deserve their success, and they therefore feel everything could be taken away at any time. One wonders if John could have survived this time in his life if he would have come to understand that people really did love him even when he wasn't in character. Certainly the John Belushi legend endures, and, as we will see in the case of Chris

Farley John had a tremendous influence on an entire generation of comics.

John's early life set the tone for his powerful drive to succeed, and it was during his youth that he began to develop some of the mistaken beliefs that what later dominate his thinking. From watching his father John learned that a man was only as good as the work he did, and John modeled this idea throughout his life. He also learned from his interactions with his mother that discipline could be avoided if you were able to make someone laugh, and John often used his humor throughout his life to deflect blame and consequences for his actions.

John also learned that one could use avoidance to escape from problems from watching his parent's lifelong use of this technique in their interactions. When people that loved John tried to talk about his drug abuse he would change the topic or minimize his difficulties, and these tools of avoidance prevented him from ever truly confronting his drug problems.

John's drug addiction had its roots in John's belief that he had to be "on" all the time to meet the expectations of his fans. Again this pattern of having to succeed in the area of work was learned from watching his father, and John's firmly entrenched thinking that he needed drugs to perform contributed a great deal to his eventual death. This relationship between drugs and performance was also strongly reinforced by John's mentor Del Close, and the endorsement of this idea by such a powerful presence certainly increased, and may have even created this faulty belief.

John's intense desire to be successful was also related to his birth-order position as the first-born male in a traditional Albanian family. John came to believe that his accomplishments spoke for his whole family's success, and this also fueled John's intense need to accomplish things. John's parents eventually became financially dependent on John, and his desire to provide for his family was a further stressor that weighed on John's obsession with continuing his early success.

John also found a sense of belonging through the use of comedy, and this was an early pattern that also affected his later interactions. John felt like he had to be funny all the time, and came to believe that this was the only thing people really valued him for. Again John felt that drugs made him funny, and in this regard several of the scenes that John Belushi was most famous for, including the final scene in Animal House, were filmed while John Belushi was high on cocaine.

In conclusion, John Belushi was a man in a great deal of psychological pain throughout his life. His nearly lifelong battle with drugs represented a war going on inside John where a part of him knew drugs were killing him, while another demanded he needed them to ensure his success. John's constant and chronic pattern of drug abuse changed him in the end, and the downward spiral of John Belushi's life was clearly reflected in the inferior work he produced towards the end of his career. Many of John's difficulties with life had their roots in the one faulty idea that he needed drugs to effectively maintain his career as a performer. This one mistaken belief exacerbated his addictions, and eventually John surrendered to the darker angels of his nature

Chris Farley

The Clowns Prayer

Dear Heavenly Father,
As I stumble through this life, help me to create
more laughter than tears, dispense more happiness
than gloom, and spread more cheer than despair.
Never let me become so indifferent that I will fail to
see the wonder in the eyes of a child or the twinkle
in the eyes of the aged.
Never let me forget that my total effort is to cheer
people, make them happy and forget at least
momentarily all the unpleasantness in their lives.
And, in my final moment, may I hear you whisper
"When you made my people smile, you made me
smile."

This was Chris Farley's code and he carried this
poem around with him all the time.

Chris Farley was a shooting star who, much like

his idol John Belushi burned out before his life and

career truly reached its potential heights. Chris was

an incredibly talented and funny comedic actor, and

his work on Saturday Night Live and in films like

Tommy Boy provided a great deal of entertainment to millions of people. Chris took the genre of physical comedy to new heights with his manic and frenetic energy, and his trademark pratfalls never failed to delight his audiences. Chris appeared in several films throughout his career, and even when he did bit parts and cameos he always created memorable scenes that were difficult to forget.

Chris Farley was born In Madison Wisconsin on February 15, 1964 to Tom and Maryann Farley. Chris was the third child in a family that also included an older sister Barbara, an older brother Tom jr. and two younger brothers John and Kevin. His father Tom was a successful contractor and the Farley's resided in an upper middle-class section in Madison when Chris was growing up. As a large Irish-Catholic family the Farley's attended church regularly, and Chris remained a devout Catholic throughout his life. One memory that stood out for Chris in these early years was watching the movie *Animal House* with his father, and, after seeing the joy that John Belushi's antics brought to his father, Chris began to idolize Belsuhi and hatched an early plan to become a comedian like his idol.

As an overweight child, Chris was teased by the other children growing up, and quickly found he could diffuse the hurtful comments by making fun of himself before others had a chance. Chris also turned to athletics as a boy, and he was a standout swimmer and later football player during his early years in Madison. Despite his large size, Chris was an excellent athlete and even made all-conference in football during his years in Madison. He perfected his class-clown routine during his High School years, and eventually took his act to Marquette University in nearby Milwaukee, Wisconsin.

Chris further developed his role as the class clown while at Marquette, and it was here that he began to develop his reputation as a party-animal. Although Chris spent a great deal of time drinking while at Marquette, he managed to graduate from that school at the age of 22, and did his first work as an actor in Madison following his college graduation.

Chris moved to Chicago at the age of 23, and began studying improvisation at the Improv Olympic right across the street from Wrigley field. Normally the process of getting on stage takes a great deal of time, but Chris was in a hurry, and convinced the club owner Charna Halpern to give him a shot almost immediately. Chris was instantly successful as a performer, and it was during this time at Improv Olympic where Chris was introduced to, and began working with the legendary Del Close. Del Close saw something in Chris, and took him under his wing and began to mentor him. Much like he had told John Belushi, Del Close instructed Chris to "attack the stage" and convinced Chris that his characters would come from releasing all of the emotions that were pent up inside of him.

At that point Del Close had been away from the Second City for a number of years, but he was eventually asked to return to direct a show, and said he would only do so if he could cast the show and include his new protégé Chris Farley as one of the featured performers. The owners of Second City, who had heard of Farley and knew his reputation for excess, were not thrilled by this idea but eventually they acquiesced and Chris began performing on Second City's main stage exactly as his idol John Belsuhi had before him. In an interview with Erik Hedegaard (1996) Farley related a story about how he found an old pair of Belushi's boots backstage at the Second City, and how Farley then wore these boots for two years in a row every time he took the stage. It was at Second City where Chris created his *Whale Boy* and *Matt Foley* characters, and while at the Second City Chris was gaining a reputation not just for his crazy performances, but also for his amazing consumption of alcohol and drugs.

Chris's almost violent physical comedy was so excessive that he injured himself while performing at Second City and missed a chance to perform for Lorne Michaels who was in town looking for new talent for Saturday Night Live. Michaels would return however, and in 1990 after seeing Chris perform at Second City, Michaels signed Chris as a regular cast member on Saturday Night Live which for Chris was truly a dream come true. While in New York, Chris who was now making a great deal of money, increased his consumption of food, drugs, and alcohol, and became so excessive that he eventually set off several alarm bells in the head of SNL produce Lorne Michaels.

Michaels, who had been through this same situation with Belushi, had vowed not to make the same mistake again and demanded that Chris either go to rehab or leave the show. Chris agreed to this, and he went to the first of many rehab stints and came back to New York clean and sober and ready to go back to work. Chris's sobriety didn't last long however, as he was unable to separate the crazy energetic characters he played on the stage with his life, and he again began to drink and do drugs excessively, in part to maintain the energy level that people had come to expect from him. Following his return to drugs Michaels arranged an intervention for Chris, and from 1992-1994 Chris was clean and sober from drugs and alcohol, but had now developed addictive habits towards food and prostitutes.

During this period in the early 90's Chris had begun to work in movies with some of his fellow Second City performers, and he had several short but memorable roles in films such as *Wayne's World*, *Coneheads*, and *Wayne's World 2*. Chris continued to work on Saturday Night Live, and his sketches, including the memorable Matt Foley piece, still rate as some of the most entertaining in the history of the show.

In the mid 1990's Chris left Saturday Night Live to begin working full-time in the movies, and soon partnered with fellow Saturday Night Live alum David Spade. He and Spade's pairing was a replay of the classic "Big guy, Little guy" motif, and their film *Tommy Boy* was a huge success and an instant classic. They would later go on to make the movie *Black Sheep* together where they continued the formula that had been successful in their previous work.

Chris thought the success of *Tommy Boy* would make his life easier, but now more than ever he felt typecast both in his work and in his life. He returned to drugs and alcohol with a vengeance and in the last years of his life Chris gained even more weight and developed a strong addiction to cocaine and alcohol. Chris continued to turn to prostitutes for female companionship, and talked often in interviews how he would like to find someone and start a family. Chris did not ever find this intimacy however, and his continual abuse of drugs resulted in a fatal overdose in his Chicago home on December 18, 1997.

Analysis

Although an Adlerian model was particularly useful in analyzing the lives of Lenny Bruce and John Belushi, this section will draw on the work of Adler as well as Albert Ellis to try and reach a better understanding of Chris Farley's life. In attempting to summarize the pattern of Chris Farley's basic convictions, some of his early impressions and the interfering ideas that resulted from these impressions will be examined.

One early impression that seemed to affect Chris Farley's life a great deal was seeing how amused his father became while watching John Belushi. Making this connection that Belushi would then become Farley's idol, one can speculate that Chris wanted badly to receive attention from his father.

This story seems a likely origin for Farley's near obsession with Belushi, and it is useful to again consider object relations theory in this capacity, as Belushi seemed to be in some kind of imaginary audience that Chris was always performing for. One normally thinks of a role model as a person that someone knows well, but in Farley's case the eerie similarities between their two lives certainly make it clear that Belushi had a tremendous influence on Chris life.

The man that linked Chris Farley and John Belushi was clearly Del Close who was a strong presence and mentor to Chris as he was to John. One notable difference may be that Chris was often very shy in his personal life, and didn't seem to have some of the natural confidence and ego that Belsuhi did at the same stage in his career. Close's instruction to Farley to "attack the stage" was interpreted by Farley as a message to exaggerate the self-deprecating fat guy motif he had already created for himself. Many of Chris's characters at Second City were a continuation of the childhood pattern of making fun of himself before others had a chance, and continued the pattern for Chris where he wondered if people were laughing at him or with him. His "Whale Boy" sketch was a classic example of this, as he played a human being raised by whales and spit water out of his head while the crowd went wild. Although this sketch was extremely popular, it clearly seems that this must have been at least somewhat hurtful for Chris to have to relive people laughing so hard at his weight problems.

Seeing others laugh at weight problems was nothing knew to Chris, as he had witnessed this scene many times when he went out in public with his father Tom Sr. who weighed in at over 600 pounds during Chris's youth. Chris noticed when others would point and laugh at his father's weight, and clearly it made a lasting impression on him. Therefore it must have been especially hurtful to Chris when people laughed at him for the same reasons as a child, and it's clear that much of his amazing humor was a compensation and reaction to these painful feelings caused by his excessive weight. The fact that he parlayed his weight into a successful career as a comedian must have been a constant reminder of these painful feelings. Ultimately he became a person who mocked and laughed at fat people, which was the very thing that had caused him the most pain in his life. This paradox seems to have made Chris very uncomfortable in his own skin, which he dealt with by abusing drugs and alcohol.

The family atmosphere in the Farley house always had a great deal of laughter. Chris and his family were quick to laugh together, and this seemed to set an early tone for laughter as a source of joy, but also possibly as a tool of avoidance. Alcoholism seems to run in the Farley family (Yu 1999), as brothers John and Kevin, as well as mother Maryanne are all also alcoholics currently in recovery. Following Chris's death the family atmosphere changed from one of an acceptance of alcohol to one of sobriety, as they have all quit drinking and attribute their decision to quit as a result of Chris's untimely death. One could certainly speculate that, because the use of alcohol was so prevalent and accepted in the Farley household, that perhaps the family did not fully recognize the nature and severity of Chris's disease until it was too late. This is no way meant to place the blame on Chris's death on his family, but instead speaks to the advanced progression of Chris's addictions, and A.A. sponsor Dallas Taylor's comment that Chris was "One of the worst addicts he had ever seen." (Puk 1999)

In this capacity, it is useful to think of the nature of addiction as a disease that is chronic, progressive and fatal. Chris was very aware he was afflicted with this disease as his many stints in rehab suggest, but in the end his addiction became a monster that got out of his control. The fact is that addiction can permanently change the brain's chemistry and have a severe effect on how a person may experience pleasure. Many addicts experience anhedonia where they are unable to experience joy in their lives as a result of years of abuse. In Chris's case when he had a handle on physical addictions such as drugs and alcohol during periods of sobriety, he would then drift to addictions that have a more emotional nature such as food and prostitutes. In effect Chris was still "chasing the high" that he experienced through the use of drugs and alcohol, and binging on food and prostitutes both appeared to provide a temporary stimulation in Chris's brain that mimicked the effects of his drug and alcohol addiction. Chris's replacement of one addiction for another should have been apparent to his drug counselors, as in Chris's case simply treating his drug and alcohol use was not enough, and much deeper insight would have been necessary to truly help Chris combat the nature of his addictive personality.

Chris's religious beliefs helped contribute to his painful feelings, as he believed that he would be punished for his use of drugs, alcohol, and prostitutes, and felt intense guilt and shame as a result of these activities. A vicious self-defeating cycle came about as a result of Chris's feelings, as he escaped his guilt and shame the only way he knew how which was through the use of drugs, which caused still more guilt and shame. Chris had serious doubts he was going to be forgiven for his activities and these feelings, which were strongly reinforced by his religious beliefs, caused Chris a great deal of psychological discomfort, and his addictions seemed to be the only place he could turn for comfort.

Although Chris was highly critical and unaccepting of himself, he seemed to have a high degree of interest in the well-being of others. Often "clown" personality types begin life tormenting teachers and creating disruptions in the classroom, as they find this is the only way they can find belonging. These personality types may eventually develop anti-social behavioral patterns, but this was not the case with Chris. Although Chris certainly demonstrated disruptive behavior in school, he eventually developed a great deal of interest in helping others, and unbeknownst to a large portion of his public gave a great deal of his time to volunteering with and serving the elderly. Chris also often spent time with children in hospital wards, and he also gave a lot of assistance to people who were trying to fight their drug and alcohol problems. In essence Chris had in many ways developed into a deeply compassionate, caring human being who had very little sense of his own stardom. Chris cared deeply about his family and the welfare of others in general, but unfortunately only found belonging with others in the role of the clown.

Like Belsuhi, Chris therefore had a great deal of cognitive dissonance in his life. On one hand he was this very hurt child who hated the fact that people made fun of his father's and later his own weight, yet he found an instant sense of belonging and even fame and fortune by making fun of this himself. This dissonance became especially powerful following the completion of *Tommy Boy* when after a critical and commercial success; Chris expected to feel that he had finally "arrived". Instead Chris felt more alone than ever, and it occurred to him that he was still horribly uncomfortable in his own skin and he again turned to drugs and alcohol to ease his pain. Drugs seemed to provide the necessary albeit temporary escape for Chris from his pain, but the guilt and shame he felt from doing drugs was also incredibly hard for Chris to deal with.

Like Belsuhi, Chris had also found acceptance from the other children by making them laugh. Chris therefore developed at faulty belief that he could only fit in with others through the use of his self-deprecating humor, and this became a lifelong belief that contributed too many of Chris's later problems. In Chris's case he only thought of himself as worthwhile when he was making people laugh. Again like Belsuhi, Chris felt he needed the drugs to maintain he frenetic pace that people had come to except from him.

While in New York, this idea became painfully clear to Chris. People began recognizing him from his Saturday Night Live sketches and would shout to him on the streets to do one of his characters. Now this personally shy and private person felt that he again needed to constantly put on a show for other people, which was a return to the early childhood pattern. Soon Chris was unable to distinguish between his characters on stage from his day to day life, and he recognized that cocaine was the only thing that could allow him to maintain that level of energy.

Chris's faulty belief system also contributed to his feelings of inadequacy and repeated difficulties in finding personal intimacy with women. Chris had difficulty believing women could be interested in him, and his experiences with women bring to mind the classic Grouch Marx line that "I would never join a club that would have me as a member." This speaks directly to Chris's sense of self-loathing and the lack of self-acceptance he felt, and explains the fact that, despite his intense desire for intimacy with a woman, he instead spent his time with prostitutes who he had to pay for sex as well as companionship. Chris's lack of self-acceptance was again an example of an irrational belief, as he believed that no one could love a guy like him, even though there was substantial evidence to suggest that people loved Chris very much.

Chris's friend Mancow Muller describes how, when he and Chris were out together in the company of women and things would be going well, Chris would inevitably do something like fall on the ground and revert back to being the fat clown that he thought people expected. This is again an example of Chris's faulty cognitions, as he simply couldn't believe that women were actually interested in him for who he was. He therefore did something to ensure that he couldn't be successful, and enacted an "I'll reject you before you have a chance to reject me" pattern that demonstrates classic safeguarding behavior. (Yuk 1999)

Again Chris's inability to become involved in intimate relationship with women stemmed from faulty belief systems he had about himself. He may have benefited greatly from cognitive-behavioral therapy which starts with Unconditional Self-Acceptance. This approach (Ellis 1999) emphasizes that a person accepts that he is a fallible and imperfect human being who will inevitably have periods in his life where his behavior is disappointing. By accepting this premise one can adopt a kind of passive volition towards life where they understand that any human life has some degree and suffering and inevitable pain that is simply a prerequisite of being a human being. Rather that "catastrophize" when something goes wrong, and dichotomize behavior as all good or all bad as Chris tended to do, people may come to understand that one's behavior does not permanently define a person's worth. The fact is, a person always has the capacity to choose to think and act differently with their life and therefore guilt is an illogical and self-defeating emotion. Judging oneself too harshly, as Chris clearly did, can trigger a pattern of behavior where a person sees themselves as a failure and then acts in accordance with this self-fulfilling prophecy.

In summarizing Chris's life, it is necessary to talk about the nature of his addictions, but also of his tremendous sprit and kindness that those addictions snuffed out. Many addicts become intensely selfish with their lives, and in this capacity drop any kind of social interest in other human beings, but amazingly Chris was a compassionate and caring soul even as the demons inside him continued to rage. One wonders how a human being so accepting of others could not extend this same courtesy to himself, as his own beliefs about his worth certainly contributed to his decline and even to his death. In Chris's case a severe system of faulty thinking collided with a very powerful addiction, and it was clear that these two forces in Chris life fed off each other and eventually came to dominate his life beyond his ability to cope.

With regard to the "Clown's Prayer" that Chris carried around with him, he seemed to get his wish, as his life brought a great deal of laughter and joy into the lives of many people. If Chris had developed an ability to see that people valued him even when he wasn't being funny, he would have almost certainly contributed much more to the world both as a comedian and as a humanitarian. Although Chris was able to channel his pain into something that made us laugh, his pain never seemed to totally disappear, and he dealt with this pain by escaping though drugs and alcohol. Chris's life speaks to the fact that, although the whole world might see you one way, it is ultimately the way you view yourself that determines your happiness in this life. In Chris's case he was never happy enough with himself to fully appreciate his impact and influence on others, and his short, sad life was in this sense truly tragic.

Conclusion

It has been a longstanding idea that the pain of childhood becomes the comedy of adulthood, and this was certainly the truth in the lives of Lenny Bruce, John Belushi, and Chris Farley. Although their respective family backgrounds were all vastly different, each in their own way experienced loneliness and rejection in childhood which they compensated for by developing an amazing sense of humor. One interesting viewpoint to consider in these lives was the role their culture heritage played in influencing their unique lifestyles.

In Lenny Bruce's case his Jewish heritage was such a huge piece of everything he did, that it was nearly impossible to separate him from his culture. His ability to mock and laugh at his own culture was a large part of his comedy, and also afforded him the ability for career advancement with the help of his many Jewish friends and associates in the comedy business. Well beyond the business aspect of Lenny's life, the idea of "Jewish Love" offered by Goldman (1974) is also huge to consider, as Lenny always felt love as an emotion with inherent strings attached which seemed to eventually invade his entire belief system.

In Belushi's case, his Albanian heritage played a major role in how he came to view his mission in life, and the Horatio Alger nature of his experience speaks directly to the pressure he felt from bearing the weight of the first born son in his traditional Albanian family. For Belushi the desire to continue to accomplish things and provide for his family strongly influenced his obsession with work, and this dynamic contributed to Belushi's addiction, as he felt drugs were a necessary ingredient for him to properly conduct his business.

For Farley his Irish-Catholic background was a strong influence on his behavior, as his Catholicism contributed greatly to his feelings of guilt which produced in Chris a great deal of psychological discomfort. The family history of alcoholism was also relevant, as Alcoholism is often a subject not easily discussed and acknowledged in Irish Catholic families, and the Farleys seemed to be no exception to this. The influence of Chris's Catholicism was not entirely negative however, as Chris did seem to derive some comfort in charitable activities such as visiting the elderly which he performed in accordance with the church.

In analyzing each man's comedy style, it is interesting to think about the different kinds of comedy and the way comedy has been used and perceived throughout the ages. In ancient Greece comedy was thought of as an expression of hostility and representing aggression (Dobson 1997) and this was certainly the case in the work of Lenny Bruce. Lenny's hostile and attacking style on the stage was a way of working out the intense anger he felt towards his father and everything that represented authority in the world. Had Lenny not become a comic he may have become involved in some very anti-social activities, as many events throughout his life suggest he had little sense of real social interest in the welfare of others. Lenny Bruce's comedy required an enemy, and whether it was the government, bigotry, his wife Honey, or especially his own father's authority, Lenny Bruce was most effective and creative in his work when he was on the attack.

Perhaps this is where Del Close's "attack the stage" advice originally came from. Although John Belushi, like Lenny Bruce, had a great deal of mistrust and dislike for authority, his humor style was most often the humor of excess as well as humor that was turned against the self. Although Belushi's Second City, and later his Saturday Night Live cast came from a very anti-establishment time and place, Belsuhi seed to find the most success in the comedy of excess. His loud and aggressive style in his early days distinguished him from other cast members, and the character of Bluto in *Animal House* in many ways became the template for what John's audience had come to expect. John's characters tended to reject the rules not through political protest but instead by thumbing their nose at traditional values through an excessive hedonistic lifestyle. In the end John was not able to distinguish these characters from himself, and his life came to embody the quote from Nathaniel Hawthorne, that "No man, for any considerable period, can wear one face to himself, and another to the multitude, without finally getting bewildered as to which may be true."

In Chris Farley's case, his humor was almost entirely made at his own expense. This kind of humor can occasionally be an effective way to ingratiate yourself to others and, at its best, is a way of showing humility and friendliness. In Chris's case his style of humor seemed to be a long standing defense mechanism that had its origins on the playgrounds of childhood where he made fun of himself before the other kids had a chance. People who use this humor style to this extent often continue to experience hostile feelings towards the self, and Chris seemed to constantly question if people were laughing with him or at him. Chris's humor style seemed to contribute to the negative feelings he had about himself, and, in one especially poignant interview with Erik Hedegaard (1996) Chris talked about how he was afraid to lose weight because he feared he wouldn't be able to get work if he did. For Chris playing the fat clown was the way he had found belonging both on the playground and in Hollywood, and he became convinced that it was his destiny to play this role despite the obvious negative consequences of this decision.

Although they all died under very similar circumstances, each of these three men took a very different path in life which was cut short much too early by the overwhelming power of drug addiction. As has been stated earlier in his work, the disease model of addiction posits that it is chronic, progressive, and fatal. Although each of these men's life speaks directly to this progression of addiction, it seemed to be their thinking patterns that fueled the fire of addictions. All of them at one time or another felt that drugs were a necessary component that enhanced their performances, and this belief in each case helped contributed to their eventual deaths. All of them were no doubt changed by their addictions, and each seemed to experience a kind of intense lack of joy in their lives which they tried to combat by disappearing deeper and deeper into the world of drugs.

Perhaps these three lives can offer some insight into the kind of personalities that are unable to simply experiment with drugs without becoming horribly and severely addicted. In studies done on the personality of alcoholics, (Pattison 1982) 6 common and relevant factors seemed to influence a person's alcoholism, and these are all interesting to consider in relation to these three men's addictions. Although this study related to alcohol, it seems as if the same concepts can be useful to other forms of physical addictions.

The first factor (Valliant 1983) is using to avoid the pain of frustration, and this seemed to be especially true in the lives of Lenny Bruce and John Belsuhi who felt intense pressure to succeed and perform, and often turned to drugs as a form of stress relief. The second factor involves using to gratify childish dependency, and, although each of these men definitely developed physical dependencies, none of them had difficulties with dependency in adolescence which is what this factor seems to be analyzing. The third factor is using to reduce guilt and anxiety, and this seemed especially relevant in the life of Chris Farley whose guilt over his activities, exacerbated by his strong religious convictions, provided him with a strong desire to flee these thoughts though the use of drugs and alcohol.

The fourth factor involves using to escape disappointment and escape into fantasy, and this was a strong force in the lives of all three of these men. In Lenny Bruce's case the last few years of his life brought many crushing disappointments, and drugs became a way to escape the events in his life that left him virtually unable to perform. Although Lenny was physically addicted to drugs for a large portion of his adult life, his addiction truly intensified when he could no longer work steadily as a result of his legal difficulties. Now unable to work out his intense anger on the stage, Lenny turned more and more to the escapism and fantasy that drugs brought, and his addiction therefore intensified even further.

In Belushi's case disappointment and disillusionment also contributed greatly to his use of drugs, and he also turned to them often to escape the pressures and demands of his life. Following the failure of the movie *Neighbors,* Belsuhi became depressed and discouraged with his career and continued to spiral deeper into drugs as a result of this disappointment. In his final weeks he became so driven by recent disappointments in his career that he began to work obsessively to return to his former glory. Again this cognitive dissonance must have created a war in Belushi's head, as a large part of him needed to use drugs to escape from thinking about his recent failures, while still another needed drugs to continue to produce new work. All of these destructive cognitions must have emotionally flooded Belushi, and the end result was that he did so many drugs, so often, that he eventually destroyed any chance of his physical survival.

In Farley's case the need to escape as a result of disappointment became abundantly clear following the release of *Tommy Boy,* and this period seemed to be a true tipping point for Chris Farley and his struggle with his addictions. Chris had expected that the success of Tommy Boy would solve all of his problems, but in fact he still had intense feelings of inferiority that he could not escape. The period following *Tommy Boy* was when Chris's addiction seemed to get exceptionally bad, and his emotional difficulties during this period seemed to have an air of finality to them. It was as if Chris had come to the realization that he would be forever typecast as the fat clown, and this realization seemed to push Chris straight back towards his addictions.

The fifth factor of use concerns using for social isolates for which alcohol supplies a pseudo-life. This factor is interesting to consider in terms of the Adlerian concept of social interest, as Adler viewed social interest as one of the most predictive traits for a person's mental health. In Lenny Bruce's case, he described his first real feelings of family as coming through the sense of belonging he felt through meeting with and using drugs with musicians as well as other comics. With drugs as their common bond, it is easy to speculate that these people may not have been "friends" in the traditional sense, but instead people who found social acceptance by forming groups with fellow users and addicts. In Lenny Bruce's life this "misery loves company" motif seemed to be especially true, and many of Lenny's relationships throughout his life were based on this shared interest in drugs as opposed to a genuine interest in their well-being and happiness.

In John Belushi's case the "downward social drift" that many addicts experience as a result of their addictions was especially true, as he spent the last weeks of his life with Heroin addicts and criminals. In particular Belushi's connection with Cathy Smith seems to represent this idea of a "pseudo" social-life, as his desire to spend time with her seemed to be based exclusively on her ability to provide Heroin and other drugs. Although it is unfair to say that John Belsuhi did not have social interest in the welfare of others, his last week with Cathy Smith demonstrates just how far into addiction he had truly drifted.

In Chris Farley's life this concept of a "pseudo" social life applied especially to his relationships with women. Chris's lifelong difficulties establishing intimate relationships with women contributed to and eventually became a part of his addiction in the form of prostitutes. Chris's last hours spent with a stripper and drug abuser was especially sad, as his impassioned cry to a woman he barely knew "Don't leave me alone" certainly speaks to the intensity and powerfulness of his loneliness. Although Chris was loved by millions of people, he couldn't believe he could be loved exclusively by one woman, and therefore spent a great deal of money paying for female companionship.

The sixth and final factor concerns addicts who become so in socially driven contexts, and this idea is especially relevant in the lives of Lenny Bruce and John Belushi. In Lenny's case coming of age in the beat generation where drug use was so widespread led Lenny to believe that there was nothing particularly wrong with the use of drugs, and this prevented his from recognizing when his drug use and addiction later became a serious problem.

In John Belushi's case, coming of age in the 1960's and seeing virtually everyone around him do drugs had a huge influence on his acceptance and continuing use of drugs. Interestingly, Belsuhi started off very anti-drug in High School but gradually began using them in part due to the social experimentation that he felt compelled towards as a member of the 60's generation. Although John smoked pot and drank occasionally during his coming of age years in his late teens and early 20's, it seemed to be his association with Del Close that represented his tipping point in the use of drugs. Having his mentor so readily endorse drugs and even inject him with drugs later in his career certainly reinforced a strong social acceptance of drugs, and this undoubtedly influenced John. His fellow castmates at Second City and particularly at Saturday Night Live were also very receptive to the use of drugs, and all of these social influences contributed to John's eventual drug addiction.

Each of these men must have encountered tremendous psychological and physical suffering as a result of the severity of their addictions and felt an intense and powerful desire to stop this suffering. This need to escape pain seems to represent the paradox of addiction, as the only way to escape the pain simply becomes to take more drugs or alcohol. No matter how many times and for how long you escape, you eventually have to come back and find that your problems and your life are waiting for you. Upon each return a severe addict seems to get a little weaker and a little less able to cope as a result of the most recent failure. Eventually, the disease of addiction did just this to each of these men, as they gave up trying to fight it and surrendered to their horrible demons. In each case there must have been some moments of clarity where they knew they were killing themselves, but each of these men was still unable to stop.

Although they all died in the throes of a major addiction, it is also short-sighted to imply that they were simply three casualties in the war on drugs. Each of these men were tremendously entertaining and influential comedians, and through the laughter they created undoubtedly made the world a better place to be. Although the three of them had particularly tragic endings, their lives also demonstrate a relationship between comedy and pain that is well-documented in the life story of a number of comedians. In many ways humor is a healthy adaptation to life that demonstrates a shared experience of the absurdity of the human condition and each of these men had a wise understanding of this absurdity.

Acknowledging that there is a relationship between comedy and pain, an interesting question arises as to the function comics serve in our society. In Lenny Bruce's case he as a comic held a mirror up to American society that demonstrated its bigotry, shallowness, and narrow-mindedness, and the audience loved him for it. When Lenny attacked the values of "society" one can help but conjecture as to the reasons people embraced this so readily, as they themselves were members of this society that was being mocked. Perhaps it is a tendency of human nature to believe that it is always the other guy who is being discussed when people talk about the problems of a "society". In many ways Lenny

Bruce's social commentary was a condemnation of not only America, and more specifically his audience, but also of himself, as he readily acknowledged his own greed and hypocrisy. Perhaps the shared feeling of our own fallibility is what Lenny was on to, and his commentary was a way of working out this paradox for people to examine.

What made John Belushi and Chris Farley funny to us seemed to involve a different kind of dynamic. Although we often sympathized with and rooted for their characters, there was also a huge element of their humor that showed how entertaining it is to laugh at the awkwardness and pain of others. In Chris Farley's case in particular the audience seemed to just assume that Chris had a thick enough skin to take the jokes about his weight, and the fact that he himself endorsed these jokes seemed to make it all the more Ok.

Perhaps if people came to understand the relationship between pain and humor they would reexamine this dynamic. What is that makes someone else's suffering so entertaining? Is it that we can watch them on TV in the comfort of our own homes without having to become emotionally involved? In any case all three of these men died much to soon as they became obsessed with entertaining people and were eventually unable to separate their work from their lives. Although they all made us laugh very much, it seems a part of us as a society must have known that we were witnessing human beings who were self-destructing. The fact that people would constantly give each of these three men drugs speaks directly to our misguided understanding of comedians. I hope this book has demonstrated how, in the case of these three comedians, this need to constantly meet the expectations of others was also a part of what eventually destroyed them.

Bibliography

Belushi, J.J. (1990). *Samurai Widow.* New York, NY: Carol & Graf Publishers, Inc.

Bruce, L. (1972). *How to Talk Dirty and Influence People* (6thEd). Chicago Il: Playboy Press.

Colby, T., & Pisano B.J. (2005). *Belushi.* New York, NY: Rugged Land.

Dobson, L. (006, August). What's your humor style?. *Psychology Today, pgs 24-29.*

E Entertainment Network (Puk, E.). (1999). <u>E True Hollywood Story-Chris Farley</u>, Los Angeles, Ca.

Ellis, A (2001). *Overcoming Destructive Beliefs, Feelings, and Behaviors.* Amherst, NY: Prometheus Books.

E. M. Pattison & E. Kaufman (Eds.), *Encyclopedia handbook of alcoholism* (pp. 517-528). New York: Gardner Press.

Goldman, W. (1971). *Ladies and Gentleman-Lenny Bruce*. New York, NY: Random House.

Gorski, T.T., & Grinstead, S.F. (2000). *Denial Management Counseling.* Independence, Mo:Herald House/Independence Press.

Hedegaard, E. (1998, February). Chris Farley 1964-1997. *Rolling Stone,* 39-46.

Thomas, W.T. (1989). *Lenny Bruce The Making of a Prophet*. Hamden, CT: Archon Books.

Woodward, B. (1984). *Wired The Short Life and Fast times of John Belushi.* New York, NY: Simon & Schuster.

Valliant, G. E. (1983) *The Natural History of Alcoholism.* Cambridge, MA: Harvard University Press.